SLIGHT VERSE

*A book of short poems intended to cause
interest, thought, and above all, laughter*

SLIGHT VERSE: *A book of short poems intended to cause interest, thought, and above all, laughter*
Copyright © Richard Tydeman 2003

All Rights Reserved

ISBN 1-84426-231-6

First Published 2003 by
UPFRONT PUBLISHING LTD
Leicestershire

Printed by Lightning Source

SLIGHT VERSE

*A book of short poems intended to cause
interest, thought, and above all, laughter*

Richard Tydeman

UPFRONT PUBLISHING
LEICESTERSHIRE

For ten years the author contributed a short poem to a monthly publication called The Felixtowe Town Crier, *and many of those poems are printed in this book. The author would like to express his thanks to the* Town Crier's *editor, Stuart Ashworth, for all his help and encouragement. Thanks are also due to family and friends, and to the editorial staff of Upfront Publishing. Finally thanks are due to you for having the courage to read thus far! I hope you will find this an ideal bedside book, loo-side book, travelling companion and stocking-filler.*

RT

Contents

The First Word
Lifetime   1

Part One – About Children
Boredom   5
Prizes   6
A Riddle   7
Reception   8
Dress Sense   9
The Soft Answer   10
Counting the Days   11
The King Conker   12
Home and Dry   13
Dolly's Name   14
Look Sharp   15
Broken English   16
Present Day   17
A Bally Shame!   18
Safety First   19

Part Two – Getting Older
Time to Retire   23
No Sale   24
Centrigradual   25
Aims and Objects   26
Short Reply   27

Part Three – A Year in Verse
Beginnings   31
Down With February   32
Valentines   33

For Leap Year Only   34
Hope   35
The Month of March   36
Oh, Blow!   37
Mother's Day   38
Patron Saints   39
A Spring Fixture   40
Daffodils   41
April Sonnet   42
Rose of England   43
Maying   44
VE Day Celebrations?   45
Midsummer   46
July the Fifteenth   47
Carnival Time   48
Caesar's Month   49
Looking Ahead   50
September Song   51
Harvest Home   52
Earlier Every Year   53
Little Summer   54
Poppies   55
A Month of Memory   56
In Memoriam   57
November the Eleventh   58
Remembrance   59

Part Four – Christmas Cheer

Starlight   63
A Cautionary Tale   64
Anticipation   65
A Christmas Selection   66
'Xmas Cards'   67
The Message   68
Talking Turkey   69
Christmas Spirit   70
L'Envoy   71

Part Five – Ecclesiastical

Responses	75
A Sinister Story	76
The Descant	77
Before the Fall	78
'Oh Law'	79
Love, Honour and Obedience	80
Fast Food	81
Age Concern	82
A Sad Farewell	83
Put Down	84

Part Six – Food for Thought

Fresh Fruit	89
Sweet Revenge	90
Rural Taste	91
True Charity	92
Sausage and Mash	93
Ode to a Whitebait	94

Part Seven – Travel Tales

Stepping Out	97
Seeing Straight	98
Egyptian Dance	99
Up with the Times	100

Part Eight – Everything Else

Guests	103
Secrets	104
Prediction	105
Bumbling	106
Perspicacity	107
Begging the Question	108
Chivalry	109
First Class Male	110
The 'S' Turn	111
A Bachelor's Complaint	112

A Fishy Tale 113
Miaow! 114
Sundown 115
Bills That Stick 116
Mistaken Identity 117
Fanfare for Friday the Thirteenth 118
White Magic 119
Right Wheel 120
Honest Doubt 121
A True Story 122
Spoonerphobia 123
A Nice Day 124
Looking Round 125
From Memory 126
Correspondence 127

The Last Word

Adieu 131

The First Word

Lifetime

Oh why do we get all bothered and fret
About time and the way we employ it?
For life moves so fast that the future's the past
Before we've had time to enjoy it.

You've come to a stage, whatever your age,
Be it eighty or eight or eighteen,
When it's better by far to have things as they are,
Before they're the things that have been.

So stand very still, make an effort of will,
And neither retreat nor advance;
But grow old with me, for many there be
Who have never been given that chance!

Part One
About Children

Boredom

'Can you remember, Grandpa,
When you were a boy,
What programmes on the telly
Did you most enjoy?'

'What, my dear, the telly?
All those years ago
We had no modern pleasures,
Not even radio.'

'No Archers on the stereo?
No Neighbours on the screen?
Oh Grandpa, I'm so sorry –
How bored you must have been.'

'We made our own amusement,
And that was where we scored.
We simply didn't have the time
To think of being bored.'

Prizes

I never won a prize at school – did you?
The other kids all seemed a bit too clever.
The same applied in sporting circles too;
I ran in races, yes – but won them? Never!

Yet now those other kids are more or less
In humdrum jobs, so far as I can tell;
While we, who used to envy their success,
Are pleased to find we're doing just as well.

We thus discover, from our first beginning,
There's no one really better than the rest.
The only prize that's really worth the winning
Is certain knowledge that we've done our best.

A Riddle

'Now, can you tell the difference?'
Enquired my little brother,
'Between a flute on one hand, and
A beehive on the other?'

I gave it up. 'It's easy,'
Said the infant with a grin,
'A flute can only give notes out,
A bank can take them in.'

'But what about the beehive?'
I asked this child so young.
'Oh, that,' replied the little imp,
'Is where you could get stung!'

Reception

Five-year-old Peter was staying
With Granny. She took him upstairs,
Then sat on a chair in the bedroom
To hear Peter saying his prayers.

The little chap knelt by the bedside,
The room was all quiet and still,
When suddenly Peter said, 'Granny,
You live on the top of a hill.'

'Why yes, that is true,' said his Granny,
'But why did you mention that, dear?'
Replied Peter, 'I reckon reception
Should be a lot better up here.'

Dress Sense

Our vicar's small three-year-old daughter,
Young Topsy, a precocious child
Would sometimes come out with pronouncements
That drove her poor family wild.

'For instance,' her mother once told me,
'The bishop came in to have tea
In his beautiful purple silk cassock,
And let Topsy sit on his knee.

I couldn't hear all they were saying,
But this much I managed to catch:
"Oh I do like your dress Mister Bishop,
And do you have knickers to match? "'

The Soft Answer

One day a man got on our bus,
A stunted little fellow;
His back was bent, his face was squashed,
His skin was turning yellow.

A bumptious kid across the aisle
Sat staring at him smugly,
Then in a loud and piping voice
Said, 'Mister, ain't you ugly!'

The man just smiled, 'It's not my fault
That I look like a gnome.'
'Well, no,' the child replied, 'but still
You could have stayed at home.'

Counting the Days

'How many days,' our teacher asked, 'are given to us this year?'
'That's easy,' said I, eagerly, 'the answer's very clear.
It's three hundred and sixty-five.' I looked around with glee,
Surely there's no other child, as brilliant as me?

But soon the smile had left my face, 'You're wrong,' the teacher said,
'You ought to listen carefully and use your little head.
I asked how many are **given**, and that is what I meant:
It's three hundred and twenty-five, the rest of them are **Lent**.'

The King Conker

It lay in Beatrice Avenue, this brown and gleaming treasure;
I'd never seen a nut so fine, (for I was eight and nearly nine).
And now this glorious thing was mine;
I overflowed with pleasure.

So, first I drilled a lovely hole – Dad showed me how to do it;
Then, whistling a merry song, I took a bootlace good and strong,
A leather bootlace three feet long
And tied the conker to it.

I challenged Tommy to a fight, but oh, the grief and pain,
My conker flew right off its lace, hit poor Tommy in the face,
Then disappeared without a trace
Down the playground's drain.

Alas, that nevermore I'll see – and nor, I think, will you –
A thing so rare and richly round, so nicely new and brightly
    browned
As that horse chestnut once I found
In Beatrice Avenue.

Home and Dry

'But Grandpa, it won't rain today –
The sun is shining too;
You won't need that umbrella,
A walking stick will do.'

'I like to be prepared, my boy,'
Grandfather made reply,
'I cannot carry both of them
However hard I try.

Umbrellas make fair walking sticks
For us old-fashioned fellows;
But walking sticks, however strong,
Make rather poor umbrellas.'

Dolly's Name

On little Mary's seventh birthday
Guess the gift she liked the best?
Yes, of course, that lovely dolly
Waiting to be bathed and dressed.

'Now,' the grown-ups said, 'Your dolly
Needs a name. You'll see to that.'
'I don't have to,' answered Mary,
'For I know her name is Pat.'

'Well,' the grown-ups thought a minute,
'Susie is a pretty name,
Or there's Margaret or Lucy,
You can choose; they're all the same.'

'No, they're not,' insisted Mary,
With her little arm extending,
'For her name is on her back;
Look, it's there you see: *Pat. Pending.*'

Look Sharp

'Do your spectacles magnify, Auntie?'
The bright little fellow enquired.
'Why, yes dear, they do,' replied Auntie,
'They help me when I'm tired.'

It was five o'clock teatime at Christmas
And Auntie was cutting the cake.
'You're not tired today, are you, Auntie?'
'No dear, I'm wide awake.'

'In that case,' the infant persisted,
'I thought it would be rather nice
If you could just take off your glasses
Before you cut my slice.'

Broken English

'Our English tongue,' the teacher said,
'We must never lose,
But there are two unpleasant words
I will not have you use.
The first of these is 'lousy',
The other one is 'swell'.
Now is that clearly understood?'
A hand was lifted. 'Well?'

'Oh, please sir,' came the timid plea,
'We always try to do,
So far as it is possible,
The things you want us to.
But you will have to tell us first,
Before we can obey,
What are the swell and lousy words
You don't want us to say?'

Present Day

Little Billy started schooling
At the tender age of four.
Harassed teacher, hot and worried,
Met him at the classroom door.

'What's your name? Oh, what a nuisance,
We don't seem to have it here.
Sit and wait there for the present;
I'll be with you later, dear.'

When his mother came to fetch him
Billy's weeping quite a lot.
'Come now Billy, what's the matter?
Are you hurt, or ill, or what?'

'Teacher told me, wait for present,
So I thought I'd won a game;
All day long I sat and waited
But the present never came.'

A Bally Shame!

Out of the mouth of babe or suckling
Often come words to set one chuckling:
Like that small boy of tender age
Who sees a ballet on the stage,
But hardly is the curtain down
Before he turns with puzzled frown;
'It's jolly well unfair,' says he,
'The men are tall as tall can be;
But ladies, to increase their height,
Must dance on tippy-toes all night!
Why can't they,' this young critic begs,
'Just get some girls with longer legs?'

Safety First

All in the April evening
There were sheep on the road with their lambs –
Or so the poet tells us,
In the old days before traffic jams.

But now, on evenings in April,
The roads are with traffic packed tight;
For the holiday season has started
With 'We've got to get home tonight'.

Though many a driver is careful,
A few treat all walkers like dirt;
And lambs – both four-legged and human,
Are the likeliest ones to get hurt.

So let's keep our own lambs in safety,
And make sure their lives are complete
By seeing them play in the garden
Instead of out there in the street.

Part Two
Getting Older

Time to Retire

Is there something you miss in retirement,
When you enter that status sublime?
My answer is, Yes, I no longer possess
What used to be known as 'spare time'.

In the past, when the wife said, 'Now, darling,
I want a shelf put up just there,'
I would answer, 'My treasure, I'll do it with pleasure
When I get a minute to spare.'

But now all my minutes are spare ones,
I no longer have the excuse.
I can say, 'I'll be late,' and procrastinate,
But it won't be the least bit of use.

When pensioners say they're too busy
To do what you want them to do,
They're not being comic or truth-economic
For I can assure you, it's true!

No Sale

When Granny comes to stay
We always have to think
Of new ways of amusing her –
She doesn't smoke or drink.

One day I had a brainwave,
This surely couldn't fail:
'This afternoon,' I said to her,
'There is a car boot sale.'

'You'll come?'
'No thank you, dear,' she said, voice lilting like a flute,
'Because, you know, I think our car
Already has a boot.'

Centrigradual

This talk of euro currency
Reminds me of the day
Our money changed to decimals
And shillings passed away.

I recollect a dear old man
Inside our local store,
I stood behind him as we reached
The cash desk by the door.

'That will be sixty new pence, sir.'
The old man shook his head.
The shop assistant spoke again,
'That's sixty pence,' she said.

'I'm sorry, love,' he faltered,
'I know I'm not too bright,
But could you kindly tell me please,
What's that in Fahrenheit?'

Aims and Objects

In our little old country village
They've gone and refurbished the pub
With tubular chairs and chrome fittings,
And now they serve hot and cold grub.

Old Sid and old Harold were sitting,
They're both of them well over eighty,
Looking lost in these modern surroundings.
I adopted an attitude matey:

'Well, how do you like it?' I asked them.
'I miss the spittoons,' murmured Sid.
'To the best of my own recollection,'
Said Harold, 'You usually did!'

Short Reply

On a wall, among recent graffiti,
Was this one in letters of red:
'The smoking of high-tar tobacco
Will stunt your growth badly,' it said.

Just an inch from the ground, underneath it,
Was written, 'Well, thank you, old mate,
But I fear that your kindly-meant warning
Has reached me a little too late!'

Part Three
A Year in Verse

Beginnings

In days of old the year began
In March, on Lady Day.

The school year in September starts,
The council's year in May.

The Church selected Advent
To give the year its blessing,

While April is the time to start
Our income tax assessing.

But while these lesser 'New Year's Days'
Continue to appear,

Old January's still the month
We like to start our year.

So, raise the glass and raise the voice
And let us loudly sing:

'Should auld acquaintance be forgot'
And all that sort of thing.

Down With February

I do not love the month of Feb,
Its showers are sharp and stinging;
Its air is like a spider's web,
All damp and cold and clinging.

For Christmas seems so far behind,
And Spring, so far ahead.
Small comfort in this month I find
And up with it I'm fed.

But though its nights may chilly be,
And though its days we hate,
Yet let's remember, thankfully,
They're only twenty-eight!

Valentines

All who are still in their teens
Know what a valentine means;
And indeed there are plenty
Who know all about it at twenty.

Later on in life,
Seeking a husband or wife,
Many remember the drill
And can sometimes recapture the thrill.

But on reaching an age like mine,
The message of Saint Valentine
Has largely been forgotten.
Isn't that rotten!

For Leap Year Only

If you're fond of February
(Not a lot of people are)
Now's the time for making merry
Underneath your lucky star.

There are, in this month unpleasant,
Twenty-eight days, wet or fine;
But in leap years, as at present,
That's increased to twenty-nine.

If your birthday this event is,
Seize it while you have the chance.
(Don't be like that poor apprentice
In 'The Pirates of Penzance'.)

One thing more: you single ladies,
Leap year day's at your disposal;
If your gentleman afraid is,
You can make your own proposal!

Oh what fun it is to play
Silly games on leap year day.

Hope

'Month of Light,' says one old writer,
Days are longer, mornings brighter;
Even birds begin to sing,
Winter's turning into Spring.

Now the snow and ice are melting,
Welcome drops of rain are pelting;
In these twenty-eight days clear
Comes the turning of the year.

On England's pleasant pastures green
New signs of life are clearly seen;
Who fears the dark, satanic mills
When buds are on the daffodils?

The Month of March

Patrick for Ireland, David for Wales,
Wintry showers and northerly gales,
These we expect and will probably get:
Weather too cold or terribly wet.

Then, in this month, though we grumble so much,
Cheerfulness comes with the feminine touch.
For here you will find, I'm delighted to say,
Mothering Sunday and Lady Day.

Maybe the really encouraging thing
Is to find that in March comes the first day of Spring.
This Spring could be short, as we see, for our sins,
A week later 'Summer Time (British)' begins.

March is a month that will always amaze:
Winter to summer in thirty-one days!

Oh, Blow!

Blow, blow ye winds of March
That churn the waves to starch
With gusts that drown the seabirds' cries
And hurl the sand into our eyes.

But must you wait until
Each tender daffodil
Has just achieved its greatest height,
Then knock all down in one raw night?

Wherever you may blow,
In France or Felixstowe,
Malay, Madrid or Marble Arch,
I say, 'Oh, blow the winds of March!'

Mother's Day

Mothering Sunday's here again;
Bind you then your finest posies,
Maybe violets from the lane,
Daffodils – or even roses.

Many of us have more than one
Auntie, uncle, sister, brother,
But, when all is said and done,
Each of us has just one mother,

She who gave, in childhood's hours,
Love we never shall forget;
Surely even finest flowers
Aren't enough to pay the debt.

So, with your posy write a letter,
Letting it your love convey;
Send it to Mum, or even better,
Take it yourself, and make her day!

Patron Saints

The Welsh and Irish patron saints
In March can now be seen:
Saint David's always on day one,
Saint Patrick's seventeen.

Then every loyal 'Taffy'
And patriotic 'Pat'
Will wear his leek or shamrock
In buttonhole or hat.

It's just the same in Scotland
When Scots will all remember
The thistle of Saint Andrew
On the last day of November.

But when we come to April,
And on the twenty-third,
You ask a dozen Englishmen
To name it in a word,

A few might mention Shakespeare,
But George is seldom named;
And scarce a rose is to be seen.
Should we not be ashamed?

A Spring Fixture

So Easter's on a different date this year.
Why can't it be the same date every year?
Well, in a way it is, because we know
It followed the Passover long ago,

Which, having neither calendars nor clocks
They kept at 'full moon of the equinox.'
This could be, by our modern counting, reckoned
As early yet as March the twenty-second;

Or else, as far as south is from the north,
Could be as late as April twenty-fourth.
In either case you take next Sunday, and
That's Easter Day. So now you understand.

The date of Easter, then, so one supposes,
Was really fixed, in ancient times – by Moses!

Daffodils

Easter time, and nature begs
To burst from buds, cocoons and eggs.
Hedgehogs end their winter's nap;
Trees rejoice with rising sap.

Now the daffodils appear,
Every bud a stately spear,
Tall and straight with leaves unfurled
To face the challenge of the world.

But when they find that Easter's there,
Each one bows its head in prayer.
This humble flower, so brave and true,
Could teach mankind a thing or two.

April Sonnet

April's the month to make a poet merry,
And versifiers love the Spring to greet.
Old Chaucer's pilgrims start for Canterbury
'When that Aprille with its showres sweet.'

'The cruellest month' another poet slights it,
And even Shakespeare has been heard to say
'The spring of love resembleth' – so he writes it
'Th'uncertain glory of an April day.'

But many smile, and on it few are frowning,
For now's the time to put away dull care
And cry out, 'Oh,' with exiled Robert Browning,
'To be in England now that April's there!'

I'm no exception to this golden rule;
But then, you see, I'm just an April Fool.

Rose of England

Saint George's Day's in April. Why, oh why?
More sense would be to have it in July,
For then the English rose is at its best,
And Englishmen could wear upon their breast
No greenhouse-nurtured flashy floribunda,
But rural hedgerow's graceful little wonder;
Its petals softest pink and purest white,
Its thorns not outward thrust to sting and bite,
But inward curved. 'You won't get hurt,' they say,
'Unless you rashly try to pull away.'

Maying

Now is the merry month of May,
The shortest month to write or say,
Appropriately too;

For though its days are thirty-one,
So fleetingly they seem to run
That hardly has the month begun
Before its end's in view.

The cuckoo and the early flowers,
The warming sun, refreshing showers
Have all too short a stay.

So let the month with pleasure ring,
Let every voice a carol sing,
Let everyone and everything
Be happy while we may!

VE Day Celebrations?

Can fifty years have really passed
Since air raid sirens wailed their last?
Since windows once more glowed with light
And fear no longer filled the night?

There cannot be a soul alive
Below the age of fifty-five
Who carried round a gas mask case
Or fixed the blackout into place.

But we, the seventies, eighties plus,
These things are very real to us.
We don't rejoice, we do not weep,
No anniversaries we keep.

Let younger people dance and play
To celebrate their VE Day,
For we remember all too well:
We've stood upon the brink of hell.

Midsummer

Midsummer's a season without rhyme or reason,
The calendar says it's in June
When days are long and the birds in song,
When the cuckoo is changing his tune.

We're at work, as a rule, and the children in school
Are faced with exams or a test;
But we know that close by is the month of July –
We're approaching the time we like best.

So while June may lay claim to its midsummer fame,
We'll accept it and not make a fuss;
But July has its sun and August its fun –
That's more like Midsummer to us!

July the Fifteenth

Dear Saint Swithin, on your day,
Our grandparents used to say,
Depended whether rain or no
Would follow for a month or so.

If you make the sun to blaze
You'll please the folk on holidays;
But if rain begins to fall
They won't be very pleased at all.

Supposing, on the other hand,
You send the rain and soak the land,
You'll give the gardeners their reward
And satisfy the Water Board.

Between these two extreme supplies
May I suggest this compromise?
A little rain be pleased to send –
But not for forty days on end!

Carnival Time

Rejoice and sing, that annual fling
The carnival's at hand,
When girls and boys will share the joys
And join the merry band.

And folks in loads will line the roads
To watch the big parade
Of cars and floats and bikes and boats
In fancy dress arrayed.

But though we care that all should share
This feast of jocularity,
Remember, pray, that on this day
We're raising funds for charity.

So hurry here from far and near,
Enjoy the sights and sounds,
And throw your pennies in the pail –
Or better still, your pounds!

Caesar's Month

The great Augustus Caesar, secure upon his throne,
Determined he should have a month that he could call his own.
His predecessor Julius already had July,
'If Julius could do it,' said Augustus, 'so can I!'

And thus July and August got pushed into the line.
(September, once the seventh month, is now month number nine.)
It's all completely crazy, but Augustus did decree it:
So August comes round every year – and aren't we glad to see it!

Looking Ahead

My great-grandma always wept
When we reached the month of Sept.
'For,' she said, 'all pleasure's done
After August thirty-one.'

Many times her tears were mocked
By a bright and sunny Oct.
Autumn, gentle as a dove,
Often lasted into Nov.

Puddings, turkeys, chickens, geese
Kept her busy during Dec.
Then another year began
Promptly on the first of Jan.

Feb and Mar bring welcome rain;
After that it's Spring again.
In September shed no tear,
Life's worth living all the year.

September Song

The carnival is over, the days are drawing in,
The kids are going back to school, our suntan's wearing thin.
So, do we sit in misery to watch the year departing?
Is this the end of happiness? Not so, it's only starting:

Ahead are harvest festivals, and then there's Hallowe'en,
And Guy Fawkes Day and party time – you all know what I mean;
For coming up relentlessly, but ever sure and steady,
We see the lights of Christmas (We've bought our tree already).

Which leads us on to New Year's Eve and into New Year's Day,
All joining hands for *Auld Lang Syne* with fun and games to play.
And after that come Valentine's and birds begin to sing;
Before you say 'Jack Robinson' you'll find that it's the Spring!

Harvest Home

'All is safely gathered in,' the harvest hymn insists,
While other poets speak of mellow fruitfulness and mists.
But, looking round my garden, I've a fair amount of beans,
Some rather twisted carrots and a few assorted greens.

The seed cost nearly fifteen pounds, the fertiliser twenty,
Insecticide and suchlike things have set me back – well, plenty.
My clever friends all say I'm just an idiot, because
I could have bought much cheaper veg at supermarket stores.

All this I know, but still I go on forking up the soil;
For just one twisted carrot's worth, a lot of honest toil.
And who can value open air and exercise and pleasure?
The real joy of gardening no man can ever measure.

Earlier Every Year

It was, as I can well remember,
The very last day of September
When children stopped me, for my sins,
All rattling collecting tins.

But caution prompted me to pause
And seek to know the Week's Good Cause:
'It's surely much too soon,' said I,
'To ask for pennies for the Guy?'

The leader looked at me with scorn:
'Pennies?' he sneered, 'Where was you born?
In any case you're much too late;
Us lot is carol-singers, mate!'

Little Summer

'Saint Luke's little summer' they call it,
For near to October eighteen
There's sometimes a phase of warm sunny days
More like June, if you know what I mean.

Now I can't guarantee it will happen;
If it does, it's a wonderful bonus.
(But if Saint Luke's Day is cold, wet and grey,
Too bad – and don't bother to phone us!)

Luke's called 'the beloved physician',
And whether we're dustman or duke,
In want or in wealth, we all need good health,
So, thanks for your summer, Saint Luke.

Poppies

Poppies in the month of May, burst like scarlet bubbles;
'Now forget,' they seem to say, 'all your winter's troubles.'
Birds are singing in the trees, bees around us humming,
Scent of nectar in the breeze, summer days are coming.

Half a year has passed away; gone the summer flowers;
Darker nights are here to stay, colder fall the showers.

Yet it seems each human soul, nature tries to copy;
Every coat and buttonhole blossoms with a poppy,
Red as blood of those who died, bidding us remember.
May we always wear with pride, poppies in November.

A Month of Memory

The month of November bids us remember,
Hallowe'en leads the way to All Hallows Day
We remember then holy women and men.

On the fifth, all excited, the bonfires are lighted:
We've never forgot the Gunpowder Plot.

Another week after, now silent the laughter
In reverence for the fallen in war.

Before the month ends our American friends
Keep Thanksgiving Day, the occasion when they
Remember, expressing their thanks for each blessing.

(A thing you and I might possibly try.)
There's so much to remember during November.

In Memoriam

The great and good, who firmly stood
In wars both great and small,
Their lives to give that we might live,
We venerate them all.

And once a year we meet to hear
Those words 'We will remember',
Then off we run, our duty done –
At least till next November.

But there are still so many ill
From shock and shell and burn,
Whom death did spare; their every care
Is surely our concern?

So though we say 'Remembrance Day'
And keep it – more or less,
Be careful lest we make the rest
'Days of Forgetfulness'.

November the Eleventh

Saint Martin's Feast has largely been
Eclipsed by our Remembrance Day.
Young Martin, then about eighteen,
Lived on Roman soldier's pay.

All his friends could only laugh
When, in one cold winter's storm,
Martin cut his cloak in half
To keep a shivering beggar warm.

In a dream that night, we're told,
Christ appeared, and thus he spoke:
'I was helpless, I was cold;
Martin clothed me with his cloak.'

Thus we learn it comes to pass,
Whether wealth or rank possessing,
A Martin or a Wenceslas
Equally will find a blessing.

Remembrance

What is this remembrance?
Tell me, what?
Two minutes contemplation
How the finest of the nation
Gave their lives for our salvation?
Surely not!

Remember War?
Out of discord came disaster,
Taking mammon for a master,
Getting nowhere even faster,
Nothing more.

What then can we do?
Try forgiving – not forgetting,
Looking forward, never fretting,
To the young example setting
That's remembrance true.

Part Four
Christmas Cheer

Starlight

Beyond the trappings of commercial Yule,
The tinsel and the turkey and the tree,
The star of Bethlehem, serene and cool,
Is shining still for those with eyes to see.

No carol is a rhyme without a reason;
The bells ring not at random, but to call;
And cards of 'greetings for the festive season'
Have largely missed the purpose of it all.

May happiness be widespread, near and far,
May Christmas spirit fill our words and deeds,
And keep our eyes on that bright morning star;
All truly wise men follow where it leads.

A Cautionary Tale

A foolish rich man, so the legends run,
Arranged a birthday party for his son.
Admittedly the son was only two –
But that's the sort of thing such people do.

The hotel ballroom hired for the event,
On preparations lavishly he spent:
Exotic food and vintage cold champagne
Awaited tasting but, alas, in vain;

For while our rich man, throwing out his chest,
Was proudly meeting each invited guest,
A voice was saying, 'It would give us joy
If we, perhaps, could see the birthday boy.'

Yes, though the wine was poured, the food all cooked,
This one small matter he had overlooked:
He had so many things upon his mind,
And so the birthday boy he'd left behind!

Let's have a happy Christmas then, and pray
That we may all appreciate the day;
But as we carve the bird and pour the fizz
Let's not forget just whose birthday it is.

Anticipation

Christmas comes but once a year –
Or so they used to say;
But nowadays, I sadly fear,
It's nearly every day!

September's hardly out of sight
When television ads
Start telling children it's all right
To pester mums and dads

To buy the latest thing in toys
(They're only fifty quid;
You haven't got one, girls and boys?
Why then, it's time you did!)

It seems to me there's something wrong:
When Christmas really comes,
The feast has been with us so long
We're only left with crumbs…

A Christmas Selection

'You just can't please some women,'
The hen-pecked husband said:
'My wife gave me, last Christmas,
Two ties, one blue, one red.

I couldn't put on both at once
However hard I tried;
So, on the dressing table,
I laid them side by side,

Then 'eeny meeny miny mo'
The red one got the choice.
I wore it going down the stairs;
That's when I heard her voice,

As always, finding something wrong
With everything I do:
'Of course,' she cried, 'that's typical,
You didn't like the blue!'

'Xmas Cards'

Two bright young things were choosing cards of greeting in a shop,
There were pictures of plum puddings with some holly on the top,
Some 'Olde English' country scenes and robins in the snow,
Old Santa with his reindeer and a lot of mistletoe.

But then, beneath a picture showing 'Elvis with guitar',
There suddenly appeared a card surmounted by a star,
With angels and with shepherds and with royal wise men three,
A manger and a maiden with a baby on her knee.

'Just look at this,' exploded one of our bright youthful pair,
'The Vicar must have dropped it on his way to morning prayer.'
The other one examined it and gave a little shriek,
'They've even pushed religion into Christmas – what a cheek!'

The Message

When you're choosing Christmas cards,
Spread before your eyes,
Is it just the picture,
The colour or the size?

Do you simply pick it up
And buy it that same minute?
No, first you look inside to see
The message printed in it.

It's just the same when choosing friends,
They're not just pretty faces.
Some people's open smiling eyes
Hide only empty spaces.

You need to look inside the mind,
For there the message starts;
And friends are like our Christmas cards,
We choose them by their hearts.

Talking Turkey

Behold the monarch of the herd,
Strutting with footsteps slow and jerky,
That quite incomparable bird
His gracious majesty the turkey!

His plumage, whether fair or dark,
Shines with a bright metallic lustre;
His eye displays a threatening spark –
Though most of that is merely bluster.

All summer long he eats and drinks,
Of all the food he takes the cream;
For he needs all his strength, he thinks,
To satisfy his great harem.

But once the winds of autumn blow
He starts to shiver – with good cause,
For now he sees the distant glow,
The shadowy shape of Santa Claus.

Now Brussels sprouts his dreams invade,
He tries to run, his breath comes puffing;
Through cranberry sauce he tries to wade,
Hotly pursued by chestnut stuffing.

But, Christmas past, he smiles to see
The tough old cock restored to favour;
For human diners all agree
His wives have made the better flavour!

Christmas Spirit

On one Christmas Eve did our vicar receive
A parcel in which he would find
A bottle wherein was apricot gin
And a challenging message – unsigned.

'I dare you,' it said, 'when your sermon you've read,
To announce to the whole congregation
This parcel you've gained, and what it contained
I shall listen in anticipation.'

But you don't catch our vicar with blackmail of liquor;
Next day in his pulpit on high,
Like an owl on a perch, he looked round the church
With a mischievous twinkling eye.

'I am grateful,' said he, 'for a gift sent to me
Anonymously but well meant.
The fruit I adore, but admire even more
The spirit in which it was sent.'

L'Envoy

There's very little more to say,
And though it may look clever,
It really doesn't always pay
To versify for ever.

So, like Gibraltar on its rock
Or Corinth on its Isthmus,
I'll now retreat and take my seat
And wish you 'Merry Christmas!'

Part Five
Ecclesiastical

Responses

The bishop ascended the pulpit,
The microphone looked rather small;
He gave it a couple of taps with his knuckle
But got no reaction at all.

'There's something the matter with this thing,'
Said he, with an audible sigh;
Though whatever he said, the mike being dead,
He didn't expect a reply.

But the people, well trained by the vicar,
Instinctively knew what to do:
As a well-rehearsed party, in unison hearty
They answered, 'And also with you.'

A Sinister Story

The vicar was doing his duty
And visiting all of his flock,
Including an elderly lady
In a highly unsavoury block.

'I expect,' she was saying, 'you're thirsty;
It's a long time before you have supper.
I've still got some tea in the teapot;
I'm sure you could do with a cuppa.'

The vicar observed, to his horror,
That though there were cups on the shelf,
The lady was pouring his potion
In the cup she'd been using herself.

He accepted with what looked like pleasure,
Attempting his horror to hide,
Surreptitiously turning the cup round
To drink from the opposite side.

He had just managed two or three mouthfuls
When the old lady chortled with glee:
'Well, what a coincidence, Vicar,
I see you're left-handed, like me.'

The Descant

Our organist has trained the choir
To concert pitch – and more,
With introits and with canticles
And anthems by the score;

Particularly putting in
A descant full of vim
To brighten up the final verse
Of any closing hymn.

A friend of mine who isn't very
Musical at all
Once came to church on Sunday
At harvest festival.

And when I asked him afterwards
If he'd enjoyed the singing,
He said, 'My word, this choir of yours
Has set the rafters ringing.

But chiefly in that final verse
Which really came alive
When half of the sopranos
Went into overdrive!'

Before the Fall

Our parish church is heated by hot pipes beneath the floor,
All covered up by ornamental gratings by the score.
Our choir is good; I wouldn't like to give a false impression;
But just last Sunday morning while hymn-singing in procession,

A pretty young soprano had a bit of rotten luck:
Her heel caught in a grating and was well and truly stuck.
With two contraltos pulling her, she gave a nervous smile.
Then slipped her foot out of the shoe and hobbled up the aisle.

A gallant tenor stooped right down and lifted up the shoe –
The heel was stuck so tightly that the grating came up too.
The baritone who followed him then took a step too soon;
He's coming out of hospital next Friday afternoon.

'Oh Law'

The vicar parked his little car
Right on a yellow line.
'I'm sorry,' said the constable,
'But this will mean a fine.'

'Dear Officer, I'll only need
Two minutes, if permitted.'
'The time is immaterial,
A crime has been committed.'

'Oh, Constable have pity now;
Has not my pleading stirred you?
I'm only a poor preacher.'
'I know,' he said, 'I've heard you.'

Love, Honour and Obedience

The wedding rehearsal was over,
The verger was closing the door
When the bridegroom came back and said, 'Vicar,
There's just this one little thing more.

'When you come to dictate the bride's promise,
Instructing her what she's to say,
Could I ask that you'll please be quite certain
You include the words "and to obey?"'

'More often I'm asked,' said the vicar,
'To leave out the words you request;
But if that's the way that you want it,
So be it. No doubt you know best.'

'Well, I don't really have an opinion,'
Was the bridegroom's surprising response.
But she says that she wants to say it,
And I always do what she wants.'

Fast Food

Our missionary speaker had a sense of humour too,
He gave us all a splendid talk on what he has to do;
Then called for any questions, and a lady thus began:
'And have you yet converted any cannibals, young man?'

'I really think I must have done,' said he with tongue in cheek,
'Before my time they ate each other seven days a week.
But then they started coming to my daily evening meeting,
And nowadays on Fridays only fishermen they're eating.'

Age Concern

The service called 'Churching of Women'
Survives in some parts of our nation,
When mothers give thanks after childbirth –
Some call it a 'purification.'

The verger came out of the vestry
At the time when a churching was due,
And saw, with annoyance, a lady
Who sat in the very back pew.

He sped up the aisle and approached her,
'I'm afraid I must move you,' he said.
'The vicar likes ladies for churching
To sit in the front pew instead.'

'Young man,' she replied, with amusement,
Next week I shall be ninety-two.'
'I feel sure,' said the verger, 'in that case,
The vicar would come here to you.'

A Sad Farewell

The vicar was leaving the parish;
He went round to say his goodbyes,
But had rather a shock when one of his flock,
A lady, had tears in her eyes.

'Now there's no need to cry,' said the vicar,
'There have to be changes, you see.
So you must be strong, and before very long
They'll send someone better than me.'

'That's all very well,' said the lady,
Despondently shaking her head.
'But that's why I'm grieving, for when he was leaving
That's just what the last vicar said.'

Put Down

The lassie was reading her bible
When two young men boarded the train;
They sat close at hand, and attempted
To attract her attention, in vain.

Then one of the lads, leaning forward,
Decided to risk contradiction,
Cleared his throat and addressed the young lady,
'I see you enjoy reading fiction.'

She put down the book she was reading,
Overlooking his absence of tact,
And replied, 'I'm afraid you are wrong, sir,
The book I am reading is fact.'

'You don't mean to say,' he protested,
'That all of the bible is true?
You can't believe that sort of nonsense.'
'Oh yes,' said the lady, 'I do.'

'But what about Jonah the prophet –
You think he lived inside a whale?
You're bound to admit that his story's
A highly improbable tale.'

(Continued on next page)

Put Down #2

The lassie then picked up her bible,
'If that's in this book, sir,' she stated,
'Of course I believe that it happened
Exactly as Jonah related.'

'But you won't ever know it for certain –
Old Jonah's been dead for some years.'
'When I get to heaven, I'll ask him;
I'll hear with my very own ears.'

'But supposing, when you get to heaven,'
Said this most persistent of men,
'You discover, on looking around you,
That Jonah's not up there? What then?'

'If Jonah's not *up*,' said the lady,
With a smile like a mischievous elf,
'It will mean he's gone *down*, and in that case
You'll be able to ask him yourself.'

Part Six
Food for Thought

Fresh Fruit

When Eve the apple first did eat,
And Adam followed suit,
They laid the blame, for all their shame,
On that forbidden fruit.

And since that day, whenever man
Has fallen, you can bet
He blames it on the food, 'It must
Be something that I ate.'

It's really time we faced the facts,
We've made enough excuses.
The origin of all our sin
Is not 'digestive juices'.

In fact the cause of broken laws –
(And this is truth profound)
Was not the apple up the tree
But the pair down on the ground!

Sweet Revenge

The chocolate box was in circuit,
I'd chosen a hazelnut log,
When something came scratching my trousers,
My hostess's ill-mannered dog.

I tried to avoid a close contact,
The animal thought it was fun;
He'd nearly jumped onto the table
When the hostess said, 'Oh, give him one.'

I needed no further persuasion,
But clouted his little backside;
With a yelp of dismay he retreated
And jumped in his basket to hide.

'I meant you should give him a sweetie,'
My hostess began to explain.
'I'm sorry,' I lied. It was worth it:
He never came near me again.

Rural Taste

It's funny how things in the country
Are misunderstood in the town.
For instance, Adolphus from London
Was shown round the farm by Jack Brown.

He saw all the useful devices,
And then, near the end of the tour,
His eyes – and his nose – drew attention
To a very large heap of manure.

Said Adolphus, 'That's not very useful,
Though no doubt it can do little harm.'
'Not useful?' cried Jack in amazement,
'It's the most useful stuff on the farm.

We use it to spread on the rhubarb,
It gives it a flavour divine.'
'No accounting for tastes,' said Adolphus,
'But I prefer custard on mine.'

True Charity

As Pig and Hen were walking
They saw outside the hall
A notice saying, 'Come inside,
We welcome one and all.'

'We're serving breakfast free today
So, if you feel forsaken,
We'll try to cheer you up again
With lots of eggs and bacon.'

'Now, that is nice and generous,'
The Hen was heard to say,
'That's what I call true charity;
 It's really made my day.'

'It's charity,' the Pig replied,
'But please don't call it nice:
For you it's a donation;
For me, it's sacrifice.'

Sausage and Mash

'Bangers' we used to call them,
And bang is what they did.
(Is that why pre-war frying pans
Were fitted with a lid?)

The skins were tight and brittle,
And often split too soon;
One had to put away the fork
And eat it with a spoon.

But, oh the glorious flavour –
There isn't any doubt;
The very best of sausages
Were eaten inside out!

Ode to a Whitebait

Wee sleekit tim'rous cowering fish,
Lying so lonesome in thy dish;
Finny friend of smallest size –
Oh, look not on me with those eyes!

Think not that I could thee condemn
An' serve thee with a slice of lemon.
Snatched from thy mother without warning
And guaranteed as 'fresh this morning'.

Oh, if thou hadst escaped that fate,
Thou frail diminutive whitebait,
Who knows? Maybe thou couldst have been
A small sprat or a large sardine.

Nay, in due time, thy little bod
Might have become a hake or cod;
Why, some small fry are known to burgeon
Into a halibut or sturgeon.

But such a wondrous thing was not,
Poor little corpse, to be thy lot;
For fate decreed thy hopes to shatter
By frying thee in golden batter.

Since fate hath cooked and served thee up,
It seemeth pity not to sup;
Onto my fork then, little whitebait,
Pull up the ladder – I'm all right, mate!

Part Seven
Travel Tales

Stepping Out

They tell a tale in Suffolk
That, many years ago,
A worker on an east coast farm
(whose name I do not know)

Decided, having had enough
Of 'backs against the wall',
To emigrate to Canada,
Out west of Montreal.

'How will you go?' they asked him,
And this was his reply:
'We've packed some bacon sandwiches
And half an apple pie;

We thought we'd go the prettier way
Through Rendlesham and Eyke,
And stop the night in Cambridge
To break the journey like.'

Seeing Straight

A millionaire from Dallas,
Whose house is like a palace,
Once drove me in a motorcar the size of a space rocket.
I was quite surprised to see,
That before he turned the key,
He slowly took his glasses off and put them in his pocket.

He said, 'You'll wonder how
I need no glasses now?
You see I only went and bought this car the other day;
But the glass they used was plain
So I sent it back again
And had the windshield made to my prescription right away.

Egyptian Dance

The tour party landed in Cairo,
Enjoying the glorious weather;
Our dear local guide came up to my side
And called the whole party together.

'Now what would you like to be doing
This evening?' he presently said,
'See the pyramids soon by the light of the moon,
Or see belly dancing instead?'

One lady spoke up and said loudly
(I don't think she'd heard him aright),
'I can't speak for my friends, but for me it depends
Which ballet they're doing tonight.'

Up with the Times

I was visiting friends in Chicago.
'And how's dear old London?' asked one,
'I suppose there's as much fog as ever?'
'Why, no,' I replied, 'We have none.'

'You're puttin' me on,' said the Yankee,
'There's fog you can taste, touch and smell;
It's like thick pea soup when you see it,
As Dickens describes it so well.'

'You're way out of date,' I insisted,
'A Clean Air Act killed it stone dead;
It came in right back in the sixties.'
The American just shook his head.

I got my own back a bit later,
When asked what I'd like to do now;
I tried to invent a good answer
Without ever causing a row.

It came to me then in that moment;
I replied with an innocent gaze:
'I'd like you to take me and show me
Where Al Capone's living these days.'

Part Eight
Everything Else

Guests

We do not love the party guest
Who comes immaculately dressed,
When asked to be informal;
Nor can we like the other camp
Who turn up dressed as tart or tramp,
When evening dress is normal.

And then there's always one we've missed,
Who isn't even on the list,
Whose name we can't recall;
While every time there's always some
Who've said that they'll be pleased to come
And don't turn up at all.

But please preserve us from the brat
With whoopee cushion, funny hat
And squirting buttonhole.
Who's quite convinced himself that he
Alone is qualified to be
The party's life and soul!

Secrets

'How does one keep a secret?'
Asked the fellow on the train,
'I swore my wife to silence, but
Apparently in vain.

She says she only told her friends
Who said their lips were sealed;
Yet now I find my private life
Is publicly revealed.'

'How many of her friends?' I asked.
'Well, as I understood,'
He answered, 'There were six all told.'
'Of course,' I said, 'They would.'

Prediction

They say that our dreams tell the future;
I've never believed it before,
But a fortnight ago, on four nights in a row
I dreamt of the numeral four.

Next morning I saw, in the race card,
The fourth race, a horse called Quartet.
A prediction like this being too good to miss,
I invested four pounds in a bet.

I sat down in front of the telly,
To watch my success in the race,
But alas for my dreams and my wonderful schemes,
You've guessed it – It came in fourth place!

Bumbling

Come now, I pray you, consider with me
That obstinate insect, the bumble-bee;
For scientists who are more clever than I
Have proved there's no possible way it can fly!

The bumble-bee's body, so bulky and round,
Would need six-inch wings just to get off the ground;
And as for volplaning from flower to flower,
The scientists say, it just hasn't the power.

However it seems that in spite of all this,
The bumble-bee flies on in ignorant bliss,
Achieving the best of impossible things
On apparently weak and inadequate wings.

And when I look round at the many of us
Who fell at the hurdle called 'eleven plus',
But pressed on regardless and ended up yet
As teacher, professor, or doctor or vet.

I remember those children not terribly clever
Whose chance of achievement was labelled as 'never',
And think of those experts unable to see
The developing powers of the bumble-bee.

Perspicacity

(Definition: Clearness of understanding.)

Some like to run, and some to jump, or swim, or sail abroad
Or punch opponents with the glove or smite them with the sword;
And some will fall upon a ball while others merely kick it;
But men of perspicacity prefer the game of cricket.

Behold the gentle willow tree beside the river's brim;
He stands up there so tall and fair, what can we make of him?
Oh, you can find a hundred things to do with wood like that;
But men of perspicacity prefer to make a bat.

Some men will take a leather skin and make it into boots;
And some there be, regrettably, who do not care two hoots,
And merely throw good leather out and use it not at all;
But men of perspicacity prefer to make a ball.

And some will take the whitest flour and make it into pies,
Or on the whitest paper they will write the whitest lies.
And some will take white metal blocks and beat them into panels;
But men of perspicacity prefer to wear white flannels.

With bat and ball and flannels all our perspicacious friends
Preserve their youth in very truth, and though their vigour ends,
Yet, man and boy, that inner joy will leave their senses never;
For men of perspicacity are cricketers for ever!

Begging the Question

Old Charlie the miser, as mean as he's tottery,
Won a large sum on the National Lottery.
I went to see him to give him a cheer
(And, knowing his habits, I took my own beer!)

'It'll make a big change in your manner of life,'
I told him, 'I know you've no children or wife,
But having this money will mean, my old pal,
You can't live like this.' Replied Charlie, 'I shall.'

'But think of the dangers from burglars and such.'
'I really don't think that will worry me much.'
'And you've thought about those begging letters, no doubt?'
'Oh,' said Charlie, 'I'll still go on sending them out.'

Chivalry

It was quite late at night when the bus stopped
To let an old lady get in.
A man who, I think, had too much to drink,
Stood up with a stupefied grin.

'Please take my seat, madam,' he blustered.
'No, thank you,' the lady replied.
'But you musht take my sheat,' said the man with some heat.
Embarrassed, the lady complied.

She sat in the seat he'd vacated;
He stood till they reached journey's end.
To the driver said he, as he stepped off, 'You see,
That was chivalry, that was, my friend.'

'Oh,' the driver replied, 'I did wonder;
I thought you were making a fuss –
Especially, too, as the lady and you
Were the only two folks on the bus!'

First Class Male

I once met a college professor
Who'd been unemployed for a while.
'Any luck with employment?' I asked him.
'Why, yes,' he replied with a smile,

'I couldn't get back into college,
I gave up my cap and my gown;
I've taken a job as a postman,
Delivering mail in the town.'

'But surely,' I said, 'that's a comedown
From those university treats?'
'Well, maybe,' he answered quite brightly,
'But it's better than walking the streets.'

The 'S' Turn

Young Margery stood in the court room
On a careless driving charge.
'And what were you doing?' They asked her.
'I was doing an S-turn,' said Marge.

The magistrate looked a bit puzzled;
'I've heard of a U-turn,' said he:
'But as for an S-turn, young lady,
You'll have to explain it to me.'

'Well – you see, sir,' poor Margery faltered,
'I thought I'd left something behind;
So I just started making a U-turn,
And then I changed my mind.'

A Bachelor's Complaint

When a girl invites a kiss
I like to know that she's a 'Miss'.
Married women have, I find,
Husbands who can be unkind.

If I know that she's a 'Mrs'
Then I look elsewhere for kisses.
Two black eyes may seem to beckon;
One black eye's too much I reckon.

But there's harder things in life:
The girl who might be maid or wife.
How can I tell what she is
If she signs herself as 'Ms'?

A Fishy Tale

When I was just a little boy
A seaman came to beg;
He told us tales of squids and whales
And how he lost a leg.

We thought of him as being like
Sinbad or Ali Baba.
His leg, he said, the fishes fed
Somewhere in Arijaba.

The thought of Arijaba then
Would haunt me in my sleep –
Exotic land with coral strand
And shark-infested deep.

I learnt years later, after school
And even after marriage,
His leg he'd lost as once he crossed
The harbour out of Harwich!

Miaow!

Two ladies (I call them 'ladies'
Though some might call them 'cats')
Were pointedly discussing
Each other's choice of hats.

'When I'm down in the dumps,' said one,
'I get a hat to cheer me.'
'Oh dear,' replied the other one,
'Oh dear, oh dear, oh dear me,

This solves one of the mysteries
That always did surround them;
For years I've gazed upon your hats
And wondered where you found them.'

Sundown

Oh isn't it fun to sit in the sun
And soak up the heat so delectable!
Well, so we were told in the dear days of old
When sunbathing seemed so respectable.

But now it appears – I say it with tears,
The sun is not worthy of praise,
For bacteria, fleas and all kinds of disease
Result from its treacherous rays.

If you believe that, then put on your hat
And sit in the shade without fuss;
It won't be such fun as your days in the sun
But you'll live to be ninety-nine plus!

Bills That Stick

I wish that I could make a law
For country and for town,
That people who put posters up
Should also take them down.

It's most frustrating when one sees
A bill about a show
Which looks attractive, but, alas,
Took place a month ago.

We don't mind posters going up,
I'd like to make that plain;
But when your show is over, please,
Please take them down again!

Mistaken Identity

There once was a man who hit on a plan
To restore an old tumbledown shack.
Entirely self-taught, his materials bought,
He began, and he never looked back.

When his labours were ended the house looked quite splendid,
As everyone gladly agrees;
And all was plain sailing, except his one failing,
He couldn't tell putty from cheese.

Now, that was all right till one terrible night,
(You've guessed the conclusion, no doubt?)
When during his slumbers came mice in large numbers
And all of his windows fell out.

Fanfare for Friday the Thirteenth

Oh no, sir, I'm not superstitious,
I walk under ladders all day;
If I see a black cat I just take off my hat
And wait till the thing goes away.

I've broken some thirty-nine mirrors,
I kill money spiders in scores.
I place little hope in the month's horoscope
And I open umbrellas indoors.

I don't think white heather would help me,
A rabbit's foot won't do much good;
But I'm bright and I'm plucky, and nothing unlucky
Has happened to me yet – touch wood!

White Magic

The witch doctor came back from England
And said to his friends and his neighbours,
'I've learnt a most wonderful secret
To put a swift end to our labours.

I saw a performance of magic,
Of course with the royal approval,
At two of the temples in London,
One called "Lords" and the other called "Oval".

Two men in white coats prayed together,
Then summoned a choir of eleven
Who took up their places as angels,
It seemed like a foretaste of heaven.

Then two men came out bearing bludgeons,
I was told they had come from Australia;
Their faces were smeared with white warpaint,
Their legs were encased in regalia.

When all were now facing the centre,
Marked by three golden sticks at each end,
The man in white coat shouted something,
A sign for the angels to bend.

Then a priest took a round piece of leather,
He rubbed it again and again
Till he had a red mark on his trousers,
And **that** is the way to make rain!'

Right Wheel

You'll find the area's 'pi r square'
For each wheel on your car;
The little ledge around the edge
Is always 'two pi r'.

The metric-minded bureaucrat
Likes all things plain and neat;
He's turned our shillings into pence,
Abolished yards and feet.

He's made us sleep in longer beds
And type on shorter paper.
(I rather fancy he decides
If skirts should flare or taper!)

Of pints and quarts he disapproves,
He can't stand pounds and ounces.
On anything non-metrical
Relentlessly he pounces.

But, thank the Lord, we've got him floored,
For be he dull or clever,
There's no way he'll reshape the wheel;
So may it turn for ever!

Honest Doubt

I don't know what I'd do without
The opportunity to doubt
The things I cannot see.
If every puzzle in creation
Had an easy explanation
How dull our life would be.

It's all the things that no one knows
Which help to keep us on our toes,
We must have room to wonder.
We have to exercise the brain,
To try, and fail, and try again,
And now and then to blunder.

From certainty I hold aloof;
Of mysteries I seek no proof;
I'd really rather guess
If there are yetis in the snows,
Or aliens in UFOs
Or monsters in Loch Ness.

A True Story

I once saw two ladies in Oxford;
They were 'doing' each college and hall,
When one of them looked at a creeper
Which covered an old college wall.

'Oh look,' she cried, 'that's Ampelopsis.'
Said the other, in voice loud and clear,
'That's not what appears in the guide book,
It says it's called Balliol, dear.'

Spoonerphobia

Said a nervous apprentice announcer,
'The thing that I'm most frightened of
Is having to introduce music
By composer Rimsky-Korsakov.

I know I shall say Korsy-Rimska
Or something that's equally weird.'
So he practised the name almost daily
Till the moment he dreaded appeared.

Then he took a deep breath and he swallowed,
'Now the next piece of music,' said he,
'Is by Rimsky-Korsakov (I've done it!)
It's the Bumb of the Flightle-bee.'

A Nice Day

'Have a nice day,' said the girl at the cash desk;
Wasn't that kind!
Why should she care for the state of my body
Or mind?

People will sometimes acknowledge my presence
With 'Hi';
Others will say 'There you go', or it may be
'Goodbye'.

But the girl at the cash desk was showing concern,
So I say
Never despise those who greet you with
'Have a nice day.'

Looking Round

It's funny how phrases we use every day
Can sometimes suggest what we don't mean to say.

For instance it happened soon after the war,
Before things in shops became normal once more,

In a BBC 'Woman's Hour' broadcast one day
I heard a dear lady quite earnestly say,

'I can tell you – in fact you can see for yourselves –
That foundation garments are back on the shelves;

New corsets you'll soon all be able to get,
Though only, I fear, in small sizes as yet;

So we larger women,' said she with a smile,
'Will have to go on looking round for a while.'

From Memory

'What was the name of those friends that we met
Last year on holiday?' 'Oh, I forget.'

Do you have such conversations as that?
Names disappear at the drop of a hat?

You're not alone; all our brains have a seizure;
Each of us suffers from spells of amnesia.

Don't let it worry you, you're not to blame;
Just because you can't remember their name.

For this you can bet, that whatever the cause is,
Your 'friends' have already forgotten what yours is!

Correspondence

To get to know a person better
See the way he ends a letter.

First you'll find it's on the cards
He will send his 'Kind regards';

This will mean he can't recall
Ever meeting you at all.

Then perhaps he'll boldly state
He's 'faithful' or 'affectionate';

A kiss for those he loves so dearly,
To the others, 'most sincerely'.

But if he writes a lot of rot
And then says 'Yours' – you'll know he's not!

The Last Word

Adieu

So now you've reached the final page
There's nothing more to say,
Except to hope this little book
Has helped you on your way.

For life can be so serious,
Like gloom personified;
We need the opportunity
To see the funny side.

May all your worries disappear,
Your troubles all disperse,
And let your tonic be to take
A little more SLIGHT VERSE!

Printed in the United Kingdom
by Lightning Source UK Ltd.
9781600001B/18